Acknowledgments

These poems have been presented over the past several years in the poetry writing class at the Renaissance Institute of the College of Notre Dame of Maryland. Many have also been published in "Reflections," the annual of that institution.

renaissance

Isaac Rehert

renaissance

Editor: Clarinda Harriss
Graphic design: Ace Kieffer
Front cover design: Carolyn Maynard
Back cover photograph: Gantt Kushner

BrickHouse Books, Inc. 2012
306 Suffolk Road
Baltimore, MD 21218

Distributor: Itasca Books, Inc.

ISBN: 1-935916-08-6

Printed in the United States of America

TABLE OF CONTENTS

MOMENTS IN RENAISSANCE
by Isaac Rehert

This work is a collection of poems that I have written during the past few years in a class in writing poetry headed by Margaret Doyle at the Renaissance Institute of the College of Notre Dame of Maryland, a program for older people.

It is not intended to be an autobiography or a memoir. I have not attempted here to reach back into moments of my being before becoming associated with the Renaissance. And there are private segments of my present life I have not touched on at all in these pages. Nor is this work meant to be a statement of my "philosophy of life"; some of the poems are even in the words of a fictional narrator. The poems are just moments of being: instantaneous responses to prompts by the instructor or to chance thoughts and events of my own daily life.

Having saved copies all these years, it occurs to me that some of them may be worth issuing to a wider audience than just the few members of our class who heard them first time around. A current letter from me to the world. Also, I think it may be a way for people who might like to know me better to become acquainted with some of the thoughts and feelings of this man they call their friend. And lastly, I think there may be some educational value in publishing them in this form.

Many years ago, when I was teaching a course in writing at the Johns Hopkins University, a newly-installed dean called each of his adjunct instructors in for a one-on-one conversation. A conscientious educator, he wished to get to know his instructors. After some verbal sharing he asked me, out of the blue, "Mr. Rehert, what is your educational philosophy?"

Until that moment I was not aware I possessed an educational philosophy, I had been working as a journalist and came at the writing craft by the old apprentice system. You just started from the bottom, doing what had to be done—the grunt work—and worked up. But now, having been pitched the question, I fielded as well as I could. "Dean A-----," I said, "it often seems to me that in college when a student is made to read a piece of literature or a well-written essay, his emotional response (probably unstated) is, 'That was pretty good stuff. I wish I could do that." Dean A-----, my philosophy is to have my students say, 'That's pretty good stuff—and I think I could do that—and I'm going to, the best I can."

That incident in the dean's office taught me what my philosophy of teaching writing was.

After my retirement from newspapering, curious to learn more about poetry, I took a course in writing poetry at Towson University taught by an old friend, Clarinda Harriss. Later I began teaching a course on Tuesday mornings at the Renaissance called "How to Read a Poem," an endeavor that has given me enormous pleasure. It is an old saw among educators that the best way to learn about a subject is to teach it. I discovered that I liked helping older people like myself, who have been ignoring poetry for much of their lives (as I had done), to find the same joy and satisfaction in it that I have found. On that same Tuesday afternoon, I attended a class in writing poetry taught by my colleague Margaret Doyle (who, incidentally had been a student that morning in my class.) This volume comprises mostly pieces I wrote for that class.

I would not dare boast that these poems are worth the name of great literature. They are not intended as rivals to works of Shakespeare or Keats. But, consistent with my own educational philosophy, at the time of writing they were the best I could do. It is in that vein that I am presenting them here. They are what they are. As I look back over them, I see that—like all decent poetry (or verse, if you will)—in addition to whatever else they are saying and to whatever pleasure reading them may offer, they also provide some insight, in an interesting verbal way, into who their author is.

Whatever benefits to others may come from perusing these works, I have found reading them again and collecting them and sorting them and having them published a stimulating activity for myself.

I cannot begin to acknowledge all the people who have helped me make the transition from first, a not very literate person, then to a professional practicing journalist, and finally to this published product of my endeavors to understand and write poems. My late wife, Ingrid Cromel Rehert, who was a dedicated painter, first acquainted me with the possibility of living one's life as an artist. Clarinda Harriss early encouraged my interest in transmuting my wordsmithing skills from journalism to poetry. Other friends—Margaret Doyle, Edith Maynard (who has long urged me to publish a collection like this), my late friend Milton Rochkind, my friend and relative Howard Maltz and his wife Linda—are mentioned among the poems. My fellow-attenders at the Renaissance have been a constant source of spiritual support. For a poet, everyone he meets, every incident he encounters, is making a contribution to who and what he is, and therefore to what goes into his writing. At this place I wish to acknowledge you all.

I dedicate this book to all those amateurs—those lovers of poetry—who enrich their own lives and the lives of others by endeavoring to cast their responses to the world around them into well-chosen and well-shaped words.

IN PRAISE OF AMATEUR POETS

They labor out of pure love alone
Not for Guinness or world recognition
They set down what they can and when done
Turn back to old lives for new vision

Not included with the famous and great
Whom they study and quote and admire
And in their fancies sometimes imitate
As they scribble and hope and aspire

They're not goaded or harassed by ambition
Not haunted by resume's demands
Enough their own simple rendition
Harvest of their own loving hands

Enough they step forward and try
To put in words what they see or recall
They're not troubled by climbing too high
Not haunted by fear they may fall

They know they're not Byron nor Keats
And they haven't the slightest intention of
Reforming the world like the Beats
They just keep penning their poems out of love

THE BIRD CALLER

I had a visit from a bird last night.
The door stood ajar and it flew right
into the brightness of my living room
as if in haste to flee the outdoor gloom

and landed on a lampshade. There it perched.
I tried to shoo it out. It only lurched
to the bannister and vanished up the stairs.
I followed, but, concerned with my own affairs

I decided, "Let it be." In jest I invited
"Make yourself at home." In secret delighted
to shelter this unbidden caller for the night
a creature from the unvisited universe of flight

denizen of a different cosmos from me
more likely to sleep overnight in a tree
than in my bricks-and-mortar human habitation.
And so I saw myself in a unique situation:

In the midst of going about my own affairs
expressing no wishes, demands or prayers
for this, I'm sent a bottle containing a message.
The question before me: "What does this presage?"

Morning, door open, and my avian guest
has fled and I tell myself I've passed the test
of a rare experience. I can truly boast
for this displaced creature I've been human host.

But during the hours since then I ponder,
"What was the message in that bottle?" I wonder—
If I believed in omens, which, of course, I do not
I'd say, "Keep an open door, it'll sweeten your pot."

HARD FACTS

What shall I write a poem about today?
The storm? The pond? The walk? The pup? The deer?
Come Tuesday and I feel constrained to say
What touches my life that my friends might like to hear.

The jaunt I took? Not one step of it exotic.
Pot holes of water reflecting clouds and sky.
I wish, like some poets, I could wax rhapsodic
Could find divinity in ordinary bugs that fly.

Could find God in an ant, in nasty mosquitoes that bite.
Oh, I do find His love in butterflies with pretty wings.
But why did He make it so moths die pursuing the light?
And make humans obsessed by the coming conclusion of things?

These lines make me see, as a poet I'll never be great
But as a second-rate poet, agree that I am first-rate.

OH RENAISSANCE
(tune of Oh Tannenbaum)

Oh Renaissance, Oh Renaissance
  We raise this chant to praise thee
Oh Renaissance, Oh Renaissance
  We sing this hymn of harmony
You make our autumn years our best
  You fill our days with joy and zest
Oh Renaissance, Oh Renaissance
  Without you, oh, where would we be?

Oh Renaissance, Oh Renaissance
  We raise this chant to praise thee
Oh Renaissance, Oh Renaissance
  You fill our days with cheer and glee
With you our eyes see wondrous things
  With you our minds are taking wings
Oh Renaissance, Oh Renaissance
  We raise this chant to praise thee

Oh Renaissance, Oh Renaissance
  We raise this chant to praise thee
Oh Renaissance, Oh Renaissance
  You make our lives a symphony
You've taught us stuff we never knew
  Unblocked our hearts, gave a broader view
Oh Renaissance, Oh Renaissance
  We had been blind and now we see

Oh Renaissance, Oh Renaissance
  We raise this chant to praise thee
Oh Renaissance, Oh Renaissance
  You help avert catastrophe
We taste of fear when all alone
  Among our friends that fear is gone
Oh Renaissance, Oh Renaissance
  Without you, oh, where would we be?

MY HEALTH IS ALWAYS BETTER IN NOVEMBER

My health is always better in November
somewhere I have a book with a title like that
it is a hard-backed book   its cover gray
a sketch of a young thin man in hiking boots
and a sprightly dog tramping in the woods
dark boughs on trees with few if any leaves
and no white covering over the bare dark ground
so I'm quite certain it represents November

My health is always better in November
I pray it holds up through this current month
since yesterday was our election day
and I was torpedoed standing by the tv
hearing how many first-rate candidates
I rooted for were most severely routed
leaving me concerned for our nation's fate
yet despite last night's returns and my despair
today I feel my health improved   for it's November

My health is always better in November
all this past summer long in the hellish heat
I felt almost a corpse   consumed by lethargy
a prisoner in my little Medfield house
handcuffed to cold steel bars of cooling vents
I even failed to take the usual care
of my sweet little veggie plot behind the house
because in my state of virtual stroke by heat
it was simply a burden too heavy and too great
just to go venturing out to water and weed
but now thank goodness it is cool November
and already my long-neglected daily walk
has stretched itself from only one point eight
to around a generous (for me) three point oh
and although inserting the key in my front door lock
I felt depleted   I found myself   no   not whistling
but with a silent smile across my aging face
I knew without a mirror was spreading there
as I heard in my mind the now-familiar words
"My health is always better in November"

THE TENTH MUSE
(for Margaret Doyle)

It's Tuesday afternoon and in we file
we nymphs, we aspirants, at our muse's feet
to place our bodies around this fount of wisdom
and turn our minds and hearts toward that central seat.

Today, she begins, she has a new treat for us:
a poet, Amy Lowell, we might not know.
But first the main event, for which we've come:
Our own poems that we the disciples have in tow.

We take turns reading, each the words of each.
Free verse, rhymed lines, personal or from a book.
For each she has applause, a word of praise
for a detail, an observation worth a second look.

She resembles her nine sisters on Olympus bred
Daughters of Zeus and Mnemosyne, his queen
Inspiring Homer, Vergil, Dante and Shakespeare
To create and nourish the soul in the human scene.

For novices like us, she repeats her perennial message
in relating deeds and dreams we should always choose
words and cadences, images and metaphors
in tune with the sacramental traditions of the muse.

The hour for us wannabe poets is swiftly passing
It's time to hear the assignment for the coming week.
She asks for nothing beyond our capacities, she tells us,
we needn't try anything in either Latin or Greek.

Just a few lines like today's poet, Amy Lowell.
"But if you'd rather write something else, then do.
Whatever you have, bring it, we want to hear it
And no poetry police will demand it be factually true.

"And if, when Tuesday comes, you don't have a thing,
if this week you think you have nothing worthwhile to say
we want to experience you, your vital presence,
So—Come Anyway."

WHO AM I?

He sat down beside me at the luncheon
He greeted me like a long-lost brother
He said he was happy to have run into me at the reception
He said he had recently visited our old friend, Albert
He said, like Albert he was having trouble with memory loss
He left and a few minutes later when I saw him standing across the hall
He looked me in the eye and asked, "Do you know who I am?"
He was quite serious, and when I said: "You must be joking"
He said, "I mean it. Do you know who I am?"
He looked relieved when I said, "Of course, you're Patrick."

I had that experience with my old friend last Saturday
I decided on Monday morning it was worth making into a poem
I sat at my desk with pen and a piece of white lined paper
I had no trouble recalling in detail everything that happened until
I reached that line that should contain his name
I drew a blank
I asked myself, "Now what *was* his name?"
I paced and promenaded around the room pillaging my memory
I didn't get it until just now, later in the afternoon
I do remember his name, it is Patrick.

A FAIRLY TYPICAL AMERICAN

My next-door neighbor at 1819
works nights and returns in the morning
when I am on my way to work. She keeps
transparent plastic covers on her living room
furniture and raises beautiful pansies along
the south wall of her house.
I don't know much more about her.

My next-door neighbor at 1815
lives all alone. I don't know where he works
or where he spends his free time. I knew his
parents but they have both died. He's quite shy
and when we pass one another on the sidewalk
and I say "Hello" all I hear in return is a dull mumble.
I don't know much more about him.

Marty lives at 1813. He lives alone, he and Tara
having split two years ago, she taking the furniture
he left with the empty house. Marty works two jobs
beginning early and ending late. Once in a while
I invite him in for supper, but he usually declines
says he has to get to bed early.
I don't know much more about him.

The family in 1811 seem always busy. He drives
a pickup with built-in polished aluminum
tool boxes which suggests he may be a plumber.
His wife—a tall strongly-built woman—I don't know
what she does. There are two teen-agers, a boy and a girl.
I suppose they are in school, but I have no idea where.
I don't know much more abut them.

At 1809 lives a large family with several small children—
I'm not sure how many—who in good weather
are continually playing on the sidewalk before the house
Neighborhood gossip says they are a Section-8 family—
or that is a Section-8 house—i.e. subsidized, low-rent.
They drive a new big black Chrysler automobile.
I don't know much more about them.

Across the street at 1820 live Charlie and his wife
Charlene. Charlie's partly retired and Charlene
works somewhere—I'm not sure where. They have
a married daughter and a darling granddaughter
named Kimberley who used to come visit them regularly
but not lately. The granddaughter must be grown by now.
They live in some other city, I'm not sure which one.

I live—alone—at 1817. I know a good deal about me
but I doubt if anyone else in the block does.
What should be clear to them, I think
is that with my briefcase under my arm
my new car that I drive to work in each morning
and my little dog that I take for a walk each evening
I am a fairly typical Twenty-first Century American.

THE BLUE REVOLVER
(for Chester Wickwire)

Leaving home to go away to school
I carried all my earthly possessions
in a single gunny sack my mother packed:
two suits of underwear, a clean shirt
a pair of work shoes
and my steelblue revolver.
Work shoes for the coal pile
I shoveled to pay my way through school.
The blue revolver?
Back then every boy in my circle
owned a revolver. At night our heads
would go dizzy with dread
if we hadn't a revolver squirreled away
somewhere within reach of the bed.

Now, about to leave home again—
this time to settle into a retirement home—
we own a whole houseful of possessions
and are engaged in picking just the few
we can fit into a single little cottage:
one bed, two chairs, pots and pans, clothing—
shirts and underwear but no work shoes—
my wife's photo albums, my father's diaries.
Everything we select will have to squeeze
into a space not much bigger
than our present living room.
Barely room for Maryann and myself,
my walker, my wheelchair and my computer.
And on a narrow shelf, a dictionary, a thesaurus
and four weary volumes of poetry.

No blue revolver.
No room inside that little cottage
to hide a bulky revolver.
Besides, since leaving the orbit of my boyhood
my brain has taken an extensive turn
and I no longer own a revolver.

Many years have passed
since I traded my revolver for those
four worn-down volumes of poetry.

ROWHOUSES

I was in my little backyard vegetable garden
checking the rows of tomatoes and peppers
I could see were almost ready for harvest.
Mrs. Sanders, who's been living next door
for a dozen years called to me over the hedge.

I was expecting a compliment on my little farm
enterprise whose surplus I always share
with Mrs. Sanders and other rowhouse neighbors.
Instead: "Isaac," she said, "when your sprinkler
is on, some of the water blows over into my yard
and lands on my car after I just had it washed."
"Well," I said, confident of my righteousness,
"it's perfectly clean water, straight from the tap."
"I don't care about that," she snapped,
"but when it dries it leaves spots and
I just washed my car and I don't want
to have those spots on my car."

Before I could answer, she began again.
"And, Isaac," she said, "when you fill that bird feeder
your birds may like having your yard
for a dining room but then they fly over to here
and they use my yard for a bathroom.
I don't want your birds using my yard for a bathroom."

I promised my old neighbor that in the future
when I water my garden I'll be careful that
none of the water blows over the hedge
into her yard.

"But Mrs. Sanders," I said, "about the birds—
they're not my birds, they're God's birds
wild, just the way He made them.
All I do is put out a little feed for them.
But it's beyond my control after they eat
where they go to shit."

It takes me longer to water the garden
these days, and I haven't gotten around
to filling the feeders. And I haven't had
a tomato harvest yet—either for myself or for Mrs. Sanders.

THE THIRTY-NINTH DAY

Oh what I'd give for a sizzle-ing beefsteak
On a red roaring fire beside a small secret lake
Still water lap-lapping the smooth sandy coast
Forgetting for now that I'm God's chosen host
For this collection of creatures, the big and the small
The male and the female, the short and the tall

I'm so sick of being boxed in this free-floating ark
Where all day ducks quack and restless dogs bark
Donkeys hee-haw and pigs oink while they slurp
Oceans of slop and then lie down to burp.
There's no meat to eat, just disgusting sane plants
Which I know doesn't matter to creepy-crawly ants

But—I'm not an ant—and

This continuous virtue keeps my mind in a frazzle
I long for some sin that would stir me and dazzle
That would tremble my innards like a loud clap of thunder
That would shake me and break me and tear me asunder
I'm so sick of the rain and that sinister cloud
I'd even blow bombs up, no matter how loud

Svelte women with sinuous curves and moist lips
Beckoning, whispering, pants low on hips
Prohibited chocolate, strong liquor to drink
Good books, bad books, just so I can think
Thoughts else than this constant torrential rain
Thirty-nine days already, my soul's in deep pain

I long to listen to music's soft humming
To tend my rose garden, to keep going and coming
Tenderly cutting and picking a bunch
To set on the table while I'm munching my lunch
And when there's a dry spell I'll never complain
I'll yell "Sun's out. Let's dance. A lovely day without rain."

AFTER THE STORM

He said that tree's gotta be cut down
I said no I love that tree
He said look at all the limbs lying around
I said yeah it'll be a job cleaning them up
He said the tree's old and no good any more
I said this block would be ugly without its trees
He said look at the way it's raising the sidewalk
I said yeah it has done that but it took a long time
He said yeah it's been thirty-five years
    I know because I watched them plant that tree
    It was the city so it's the city's tree
He said I've called and told them to cut it down
    They said because it's in front of your house
    You're the one who has to ask them
I said if it's their tree
    then maybe they'll come and just trim it
He said it's up to you
    but you need to tell them to cut it down
    'cause next time stuff might damage a car
    or else fall on the house
I said yeah I'll call them in the morning
He said call them and tell them to cut it down
I said yeah I'll call them in the morning

Later after their office opens I'll call them

    and ask them to come trim the tree

29

ELEGY FOR RALPH

I remember the bounce
like a compact rubber ball
striking the ground
and coming straight back at me
sometimes surprising me
before I could set my hands
in position to catch it

The easy smile, the wry laugh
of a a boy at peace with himself
the way he attacked his assignments
as he must have watched his officer-father do
eyes glued to his quarry
eager as a hound on track
only with a grin and a final
it's-not-that-important chuckle
after he was done or else had to confess
he was giving up the chase

Respectful but never in awe of us teachers
he dutifully performed what was asked of him
never complained about it
and in return let us know
what his own expectations were

He went on to a career as a lawyer
to marry his college sweetheart
and father a family
and it was my privilege later
as a former teacher
to have an occasional meal with him

True to his old self, he said (correctly)
"Mr. Rehert   you were a good math teacher
but you were a lousy French teacher."

Ralph, you were not my biological child
and I was not your biological parent
but as my student

you were a kind of son
and I regret that as your teacher
I did not convey to you successfully this lesson:
It is not right, it violates everything sacred
for a father to have to have to bury his own son

LIGHT RAIL

Let's take a ride together, just you and I
I already feel motion and don't need to ask why

Through the woods we are off on a shiny steel track
Between houses, tall buildings, with a clickety clack

Industrial, residential, we ride beside highways
At times we're enticed by sight of chic byways

On the parallel track, another train is approaching
It's bellicose bumper breathes, "Don't even think of encroaching."

Slowly round a curve a blood-curdling squeal
Like an animal trapped—it's just steel grating steel

A signal light for our driver, on-and-off blinking red
She cuts back our speed, not quite sure what's ahead

At each station a sign, ultra-blue round a yellow disc
A train-image warning, "Near the track at your own risk."

A park-and-ride lot, autos lined up, all at rest
Their owners proclaiming, "Public transport is best."

After Lutherville, no stops, we're off at a fast clip
Now trees, sheds and people have become just a blip

In the valleys we fly, we soar and we leap
But we slow down for bridges, crossing them at a creep

At last we approach where we were aiming to go
At the high price of gas, we've saved a bit of dough

Now we alight, it's at our stop on the way
Thanks for a nice ride, let's have a nice day.

ON THE INSIDE
(the prayer of Jonah)

Lord,
It *is* noisy in this cave: same ruckus
as the market place in town: vendors screaming
fishwives bawling, brassy jazzmen rocking
and rolling. So loud—I hope I'm only dreaming.

And black. Lord,
This black beats the dreariness of pitch.
No sun enters here. No moon. No star.
Not one window to let a crowing rooster in.
No candle to brighten the gloominess of tar.

Lord,
could this place be a jungle I am in?
Is that shriek I hear a troop of monkeys wheezing?
That thunder a pair of hungry hippos belching?
And those cyclones—are they ailing aardvarks sneezing?

Or is this a circus—trained animal commotions?
Loud explosive popping of gas balloons
bubbling blithely in a jabbering brook—
is that an act of friendly tame baboons?

I just heard something like an atomic bomb—
culmination of smart soldiers' art.
Scary. Was that outburst made by man?
Could that be just leviathan's healthy fart?

Lord,
what am I to eat in this forsaken desert?
I reach for bread; it hisses at me and growls.
I touch a rounded stone I think's an egg
And it turns round and snarls at me and howls.

And, Lord,
Besides the noises and the dark there's stench
Of carcasses digested and half-rotten.
Foul mush and sludge about to turn to shit—
Food eaten weeks ago by now forgotten

Lord,
I give up. You win. You commanded, I said "No."
But the strength of my resistance did not prevail.
You ordered me, "Sail north," but I sailed south
And so you had me swallowed up (or was it down?) by a whale.

Now, Lord,
You win. I surrender. You're the boss.
I did it my way, I had my youthful fling.
From this day forth I'll do whatever you command
You are my king.

NEAR

Across the table from me
I see nothing but the narrow bare neck
exposed between the slender chin
and the gauzy summer blouse.

So white, so tender, so fragile.
Like a newborn baby's thigh
a piece of ancient brittle China
or fine Venetian glass.
Anything—a brute
or a mishap—could so easily break it.

The dinner talk is of the weather, of politics, of love
but my attention, my thoughts, my eyes
are all unmoved from that bare white fragile neck.

At this stage of old age
regretfully
I suppress any desire to possess it
to explore it
even to caress it.

Enough for me its closeness
its youthful beat
like a hummingbird's quivering wings.
The nearness of its throb-throb-throbbing pulse.

INHERITANCE
(for Edith Maynard)

With your cardboard suitcase
and your black bag
full of your brother's socks
you were extremely fortunate!
I didn't inherit anything.

Only memories of a family
struggling together
during the Depression.

But I was too young
to know about the struggling.

How they all made happy
times for the little sister
and daughter
is beyond
my comprehension.

LEGS

In the lobby of the suburban church
I noticed—
though I didn't get to meet their owner—
surrounded by chattering friends
a tall young woman
with long shapely legs
in silken hose that glowed like polished gold
balanced on high heels
her short skirt skipping just midway
over statuesque well-formed thighs.

In that somber-clad Sunday crowd
she blossomed like a rose in a weed patch.
No one else seemed to notice
though I'm convinced others couldn't fail to do so.
I did not get to talk to her
even to learn her name.

In proper time the preacher and his pious flock
confessing their sinfulness
their imperfections
offer praises to their maker
for his blessings this fresh spring morning.

Beautiful lady
ignore them.
Those precious golden legs of yours
were blessings that surpassed them all.

Both women and men
sitting later with cocktails in their country clubs
will grow misty-eyed remembering
the way you floated through that church foyer
offering up your glistening jewels
on levitating wings
that made their glow even brighter.

No need for another prayer.
Of the memories of this sunny morning
in that consecrated place
you with your gorgeous golden gift
remain praise enough.

THE CAFE GOLDEN WEST

I enter the joint they call Cafe Golden West
She is standing near a cowboy who is drinking
Her eyes are black coals, her skin is fresh snow.
This ripe peach is for me, I am thinking.

"Bartender, two." I hold one out her way.
"Fair lady, will you sit down with me?
I've roamed all over this ocean of gold
And never a beauty like you did I see."

I ask her her name. She says, "Maegold N. West"
She never bothers asking me mine.
Her eyes whirl like pools to the back of the bar
Something tells me she is flashing a sign.

"Are you waiting for somebody else?" I ask
I'm marshmallow when it comes to a fight.
But oh, those black eyes and that snow-white skin
The heart insists plunging forward is right.

I brush her jeweled hand, her Avon-rouged cheek
My voice is beginning to stutter
I can't recall ever knowing rapture like this.
"I'm ecstatic with true love," I mutter.

Her glass empty now, fiery eyes turn to ice
"Bud, unless you're bucking for battle—
That bozo at the bar making a beeline this way
Is saying, buddy, you'd better skedaddle."

With my heart split in two, my nose still in one piece
I make tracks from the Cafe Golden West
But, oh those eyes like black coals, that skin of white snow—
Well—read my book if you want to learn the rest.

HOW I SPENT MY SUMMER VACATION

I called her my little mermaid
on my vacation by the lake.
Swimming, sailing, windsurfing—
those aquatic sports that make
a denizen of the sea
seem princess-like to me.

I helped her paint her boat
and carry it to the shore.
She captained, I was crew.
I recalled that in fairy lore
the maiden saved the prince
and she's loved him ever since.

I was about to e-mail home
I'd be giving up my job.
This pretty little sea maid
was just about to rob
me of my better sense.
My brain was getting dense.

But

Then one day it rained.
The maiden and her beau
forced to stay indoors
let stories from inside flow.
A lovely unreal sprite
and a bookworm erudite.

Rides on tortoise backs.
Dolphins she's been racing.
Eluding jaws of sharks.
A far differet kind of pacing
from a teacher teaching kids
how to distinguish don'ts from dids

My two-week vacation passed.
My ticket on the plane

I never called to cancel.
Back home I did not explain
The good times that I had
and skipped mention of the bad.

VALENTINE

Nobody at our house ever hugged—
not to mention kissed—
even on Valentine's Day.
I can't ever remember Poppa
wrapping his arms
around Momma's sickly shoulders
and the only time I ever felt them on mine
was when I was suffering from croupe
and he had to carry me
gasping for breath
outside to the cab
to get me to the hospital.

Life for our immigrant family was hard
and Valentine's Day was just another day—
a foolish Gentile holiday—
when we children in school played games
cutting out hearts in art class
from colored heavy red paper
and then pasting them on lighter cardboard
and with colored crayons
spelling out the words
"Be My Valentine"
even though we weren't sure what they meant.

Now as an adult I am still shy
and uncomfortable
about how to behave on Valentine's Day.
If you were here I'd probably present you
with a red-hearted box of chocolates
even though I knew they were bad for you.

But you are far away
and there isn't time to mail a red-hearted card.
But today we have instant e-mail
and no longer the child
I am taking advantage
of this advantage we have
and as my adult self
I wireless these words
I now understand:
BE MY VALENTINE

VOICES

A voice within is telling me to call you—
to hear your voice on the wire—
your words   your humor   your being—
to fill the emptiness
that so often gapes
beneath the gates of my heart.

But I refrain
I do not call

as I refrained
from calling you yesterday
when I was traveling
although then too
I heard the same voice within.

This yearning—
just to hear your voice—
surfaces from some deep place—
wordless—
while the red flag
that shouts, "Wait, not yet"
arises conscious and clear
lodged in words
I understand only too well.

It says, "Go easy, Isaac
go easy
you are engaging with a soul
that has been wounded—
are there any other kinds?—
a soul in the process of healing.
Go easy. A wounded soul
needs its space."

Sensitive? Yes, but also
from somewhere
I hear a second voice promising
that when another day passes

without your having heard from me
you may share a similar yearning
to have me touch you
through my voice on the wire—
or perhaps in person.

ONCE AGAIN
(a sort of cento for autumn)

Once again we're in
   the season of mists and mellow fruitfulness

I never thought I'd ever be grateful
   to see again those weary bent-over cornfields

Think! These darkening days of autumn
   are actually as beautiful as days can be

And that time of year that mayest in me behold
   when yellow leaves... oh, you know...

So, come, let's go down the road together—
   just you and I—
   go hunting for that romance that last time passed us by

At Shreve high school when autumn Saturdays
   were just for football games
   for rooting that our team win or lose

What did we know?

And now   behold we're fortunate enough
   to have autumn once again

So let's you and I this time go down the road together
   where the red leaves fly
   not long before the coming of the snow

Cares will drop away from us
   like those leaves blown out of trees

This time we'll leave football
   with other toys of childhood
   at the high school

And as we go
   lest our grandchildren think we seem too old
   we can always wear the trinkets we had saved for them

AWE

(Awe: an emotion of mingled *reverence, dread* and *wonder* inspired by something majestic or sublime—American Heritage Dictionary)

Wonder:
I am a man devoted to words, but words are failing me. How do I adequately express my feelings as, driving routinely along Route 83 on a golden October afternoon, I am confronted by the gorgeous color of the trees beside the highway. The unbroken tapestry of varying reds, greens, russets, umbers, browns. Over the purring of my engine and the hum of cars rushing by me, I try to imagine who or what is responsible for all that colorful beauty: the oaks, the maples, the beeches, the sassafras. The wonder in this part of the world of the annual change of the seasons. And where did esthetic sensibility evolve from?

Dread:
Words fail me again, as, continuing along the highway, I recall the news that Pete, a friend, a colleague, a fine sweet human being, has just died and that his funeral will be held on Thursday. Grand elegies have been penned, and thick books of philosophy published by great minds trying to cope wth the meaning, or meaninglessness, of what this is all about— this abrupt cessation of all the things represented by Pete's brief sojourn on Earth: the people he loved and those who loved him, the things he liked to do, his teaching, his interest in poetry, his music.

Reverence:
And words fail me once again, as continuing on my way, lightly holding the steering wheel, my foot gentle on the accelerator, I am enjoying the colors, the sparkle of autumn nature while simultaneously seeing images of my friend—his perpetual look of surprise, his occasional stutter, his openness, his warmth—and witnessing his recent demise. And understanding and accepting that my fate—and that of all of us—will inevitably be like his. And it comes to me with some feeling of admiration and respect that somehow, I, a simple aging Twenty-first Century Man, pursuing his daily chores on this golden afternoon, can simultaneously sustain these two types of awe in a mix of harmony and devotion within the infinity of his human soul.

A DELICIOUS MOMENT

A sudden flash.
  A gate locked
    to shut down the heart
      unpremeditatedly
        bursts open.

A firefly
  in the obscure warmth
  of a summer's night
    simply flashing
      its momentary message.

A star
  newborn
    in the infinite vastness
      of eternity
        simply lighting up.

No point
  in asking
    where from?
      or why?
        or for how long?

Simply flashing.
Simply lighting up.
Bursting open.
"Here am I."
"Where are you?"

IWTIAL
(for Joyce)

The characters stand up boldly
mysteriously—on the Mercedes
license tag—black letters on white—
brightly—eye-catchingly—illuminated
in the glare from the tall sidewalk lamp.

        IWTIAL

I slide the ends of my fingers over
the smooth ridges of the raised letters
—some gritty road-dust wipes off—
and to my friend I say, "You must be
intending to send a message."

        IWTIAL

"Yes, I am—I won this expensive car
in a lottery at the place where I work
and I want everybody to know
that I'd never be driving and owning
this fancy a car if I hadn't won it in a lottery."

        IWTIAL

I want to send the same message: I W T I A L
With my computer I will make an ID
similar to the ones we wear at conferences.
Like my friend I want everybody to recognize
the valuable treasures I won in a lottery.

        IWTIAL

I'll wear this ID on various parts of my body
to announce: my physique—still healthy
my heart—still beating strong for my age—
my eyes—still seeing but not what they were.
All qualities I won in a lottery.

IWTIAL

I think my chest is the place to wear the ID
to declare my spirit—still hungry for life
still able and willing to give and get love—
at this late date better than ever.
Aspects of spirit that I won in a lottery.

IWTIAL

And everything surrounding my birth—
the who? what? where? why? and how?—
that although my parents were immigrants
they were legal and so we weren't persecuted.
That bit of happy fate I won in a lottery.

IWTIAL

Sometimes when I survey the scene around me
I wonder why Jack isn't caring better for his body
as if he feels no joy in staying alive
or in accepting and reaching out for love.
What a losing ticket he drew in the lottery!

IWTIAL

Sometimes when I get to feeling self-important
and imagine my body, my mind, my spirit
are possessions I created all by myself
I'll cast eyes to the ID I'm wearing and recall
the message on my friend's Mercedes.

IWTIAL

As   h a thunderous roar
An   for an hour that's a bore

She   good stuff to buy.
Ther   n and a sigh.

She l   a fat wad of dough
Whic
Her c   ned and low.

No m   ing the time.
So wh   idn't a dime?

She'll h   sweet things she tasted
And ca   ood while they lasted."

Now ar .... aircraft is reaching its port.
Put those pages away. It was good while it lasted.

(handwritten, vertical:) RENAISSANCE

(handwritten:) to 2 to o

HOLIDAY DINNER

Avocados Vero-Nica in Aeolic aspic
Breast of bullfrog in beef-bouillion boiled
Chilled chicken breast with chihuahua chili
　For this dinner we have deliriously toiled

Diamondback legs with artichoke dumplings
Ewe stew with garnish of beets
Frankfurters fresh from the French boucherie
　With oodles of french fries called frites

Groin of giraffe charcoal-grilled to look golden
Ham in huge hunks, lean and lardluscious
Impala inundated in iodized salt
　A holiday banquet that's precious

Jello in five flavors on the halfshell
Ketchup coiled and clotted in cloth-covered jars
Kidney beans curdled in blackstrap molasses
　You'll be glad for a drink at the bar

Low-sodium squash squirreled away in square boxes
Manhattan-cocktail Maraschino cherries
Nuts of all kinds—from almonds to zilbranuts
　Washed down with juice of strawberries

Oranges orotund oozing with juices
Peas and pumpkins together pureed
Quince quick-fried with jellied quinoa
　You will wish for this dinner you'd stayed

Raspberries roasted with rare tongue of house mouse
Sow-belly in sweet-and-sour soy
Tomatoes toasted in tartary sauce
　That won't sully this day of pure joy

Undercooked broccoli barley and black beans
Veggieburgers, broiled and half-baked
Wild salmon netted just today in the think tank
　No farm-raised, we want nothing faked

Xisophuran steamed just like Maryland crab
Yorkshire-terrier pudding—hearty and healhy
Zebu-hump sections sliced thin and deep-fried
  Such victuals are not just for the wealthy

This is the stuff of our Holiday feast
That it's nourishing isn't the question
From ambrosia-eria to zucchini-eria
  Guaranteed to give indigestion

CURBSIDE DRAMA

He sits down on the curbside bench
beside me

"I guess there's room for another body
to rest here"

He is old and black and as he settles in
I hear a tired sigh

Side by side we sit in silence watching
the tide of traffic coursing by

By his left side he has set down
a black canvas bag

His right hand rests on the curved head
of a sturdy wooden cane

Wordless together we sit watching the tide
and then he stands up

In his left hand he is holding his black
canvas bag

As he walks forward his slight weight shifts
toward his right

And then laboriously he lets it settle onto
the curved head of his cane

"It's been a beautiful day." One wordless
glance back before he steps off the curb

Such is the natural attraction between Men
—when not misdirected—

that my eye will not abandon his slight
arched back

as he slowly carefully threads his way
through the tireless tide of traffic

and lets it go only after it reaches the safety
of the pavement at the other side

ALCHEMY

When I consider the many Halloweens
I've skylarked in—dressed like a red-nosed clown
floppy steamboat shoes, mustaches of burnt cork
face of evil under a leering kingly crown

When I watch children soaring like birds airborne
on skateboards over bumpy urban ground
then suddenly transformed to bony frames with fangs
to frighten spirits with devilish look and sound

And when, despite my serious adult woes
I still can hear the clarion call resound
of reveille for saints in ghoulish graves
my pulses leap and my heart begins to pound

Such is the alchemy of this holiday of joy
that transmutes a somber older man into a fun-filled boy

OLD GUYS REUNION

We've just finished having lunch together
  and, missing you, already I'm asking
  when will I see you guys again?
Our committee had gathered to plan our 70th
  high school reunion—which means
  we're all 88, give or take a year or so
And we all look it

There's Randy, with your two artificial knees
  and your back bent into a U-shape—
  I'd never have recognized you elsewhere
There's Ted, wearing the same pert bowtie
  as ever but now you've added wrinkles
  around your eyes and a blond hairpiece
There's Tom, still gargantuan but now bald
  you were a star on the varsity football team
  and I felt intimidated to be around you
There's William, you always wore such elegant
  jackets and ties that I in my Depression duds
  considered you someone from another planet

I wonder if you guys ever took any notice of me
  so quiet, so shy, so intimidated by your clothes
  your outgoingness and your excellent manners
Was I the only one of those hundreds of fellow-students
  who admired you and felt envious
  who wished we could be walking in your shoes
No, I don't think I was the only one

Now, here we are together
  bonded by the age bracket we happen to be in
  and by that chunk of history we lived through together
What a shame it's taken me—us—so long
  to appreciate the beauty of those years
  our youth, our vitality, our first flowering to the world
Nothing really to be scared of
  nobody to be envious of
  just other kids learning to be in the world

Coming together to plan a reunion
 for fellow members of our class

I'm grateful we've had this opportunity to come together
 that the gates that used to be closed have now opened
 that I am still here to come together again with you guys

And when will I see you guys again?

Will I ever see you guys again?

THE NEW YORKER MARCH 16, 2009

Glossy pages displaying the most beautiful
women in the world in sophisticated dark-hued
eyewear by Prada. Pouting lips between dangling
Douglas earrings certain to be solid gold.

Luxury ads: "Indulge without splurging."
Cartoons revealing the absurdity of ourselves.
Reviews of books, art, music, politics—
all the trimmings that make a life worth living.

And then—five pages of Updike. His portrait.
His final poems as he faced his oncoming end.
A mind that encompassed it all—sex, love, art, God

the approach of Death. Nothing eluded it.
And today, in these same glossy pages
among the other luxuries, his monument.

MASSACRE IN THE SCHOOLHOUSE

The driver parked his truck and said
"I'll work no more today.
Today I'll avenge my daughter's death
and I'll do it in my own way."

He fetched his gun from its hidden slot
underneath a bale of hay.
He loaded it with a dozen shells
he'd been saving for just this day.

He drove to the local schoolhouse where
children learned to read and write
burst into the class waving his gun
"I know what's wrong and what's right

"It was wrong of God to steal my kid
the center of my everyday joy.
It was wrong of him to take her life
as if she were a painted toy.

"It's clear that God smiles on these kids
They're happy as my kid might be.
I know what's right. I'll get even now.
Just wait and the world will see."

He lined a dozen girls against the wall
fired his pistol at them and then
aimed the muzzle at his own curly head
and pulled the trigger again.

The fathers of the village gathered and wailed
"How could this outrage befall us?
Crimes like this only happen to kings
where murders are committed in a palace"

The village mothers to his family and wife
said "What misery your man must have known
to be so angry at God as to punish Him
by killing others in revenge for his own.

58

"What misery you and yours must bear
for what seems unforgivable madness.
But let us forgive and seek to understand
and with God's help deal with our sadness.

"People get sick—their backbones, their lungs.
We don't judge for physical ailing.
They also get sick in their brains, in their souls
Let's not condemn for such failing."

A great nation watched and felt their tears flow
as their hearts in deep sorrow awoke
and pondered the message of peace and love
being taught by these simple folk.

HOW TO WRITE A POEM

Paper clips, fat cue tips and other things ippy
A teacup that's cracked, making my desktop all drippy

Eyeglasses, theater passes, snaps of pretty lasses—
He remembers them young as students in his classes

An empty bottle from milk, an old scarf made of silk
You can create a poem out of junk of this ilk

Ball-point pens, images of hens, changes of tenses—
You can't predict when, but this will blow out your senses

Practice, determination, keeping your nose to the stone
It may seem a waste, but you're never alone

The poet has always liked to tickle his brain
He thrives on the challenge of a strong verbal strain

He says it's rewarding, when the long day is done
Like   going outside in the cold for a run

And the next day, where the jock stays in bed cause he's tired
The poet darts up with a spring cause he's wired

He reads his own words and with zing shouts "Doggone it
It's really a poem. And it's I who have done it."

ECHO

On a trip to the beach by the ocean last summer
I was looking for creatures washed up by the tide
when all of a sudden there rose up before me
a lonely beached whale that was trying to hide

Its color was black and white, its flippers were dowdy
its breathing hole snored like a wind in a storm
Its fluke smacked the sand like a fan in a crater
In every single feature it conformed to the norm

I wasn't quite sure what the right thing to do would be
To call the police, the beach boys—or just wait.
To lift it and slide it on its back to the sounding surf
Daunted my soul, I had to leave it to its fate

Later I learned that beached whales were no rarity
This one, named Echo, was not one of a kind
But this Echo was here, at my feet, warm and breathing
So this Echo still remains in my mind

TROCHEES

Kansas, Texas, You Ess of A
States that are trochees, visited today
England, Iceland, Portugal too
Nations of Europe, you're trochees too

Travel's a joy when you're young and still able
When old, pass it by; keep your horse in the stable—
But wait! I've lost track of my poem with a trochee!
This is getting bizarre—I must stop—it's too hokey

Where do you find common words that begin
Boom at the start, *boom-da* as they spin
Men and women, thought and song
Into poems short and long?

Start in Kansas, delve the dictionary
Wander the East Coast, plod the prairie
Search for scarce trochees, *boom-das* rarely sung—
Forget it, they're too far from the heart of our tongue

RULES AND REGULATIONS
(a villanelle)

Rules and regulations are iron bars that jail the heart
Turning adults into children drilling lessons learned in school.
Break loose, run wild, chase your feelings off the chart.

Real life only comes when you've been pierced by Cupid's dart.
Dismissing love and romance is the posture of a fool.
Rules and regulations are iron bars that jail the heart.

Wondering *if* and *may I* makes it sure you'll stay apart.
Asking for permission, you're still a child, an adult's tool.
Break loose, run wild, chase your feelings off the chart.

You're been taught the proper way to be is very smart,
That passion felt by old folks is a thing no longer cool.
Rules and regulations are iron bars that jail the heart.

Declaring love is to restore the horse before his cart
While keeping still about it is a child stuck on his stool.
Break loose, run wild, chase your feelings off the chart.

Go ahead, *carpe diem,* It's not too soon to make your start.
The water isn't cold, go ahead—jump in the pool.
Rules and regulations are iron bars that jail the heart.
Break loose, run wild, chase your feelings off the chart.

WITHOUT KNOWING
(a pantoum)

I'm jealous of the birds, the trees, the streams
They know what they know without knowing
They fly, pierce the sky, ramble a course to the sea
While we plod unpeaceful in the unknowing city

They know what they know without knowing
No need for research or learned books
While we plod unpeaceful in the unknowing city
Yet we claim we're the culmination of creation

No need for research or learned books
They dance like sprites to rhythms only they can hear
Yet we claim we're the culmination of creation
Living among them I long to know what they know

They dance like sprites to rhythms only they can hear
They fly, pierce the sky, ramble a course to the sea
Living among them I long to know what they know
I'm jealous of the birds, the trees, the streams

NOW THAT YOU'VE GOT IT, FLAUNT IT
(a villanelle)

This is something you've always wanted
To be yourself—both the dark spots and the bright.
Now that you've got it, flaunt it.

As a child you were forever being daunted
Your talents obscured in shades of night.
This is something you've always wanted.

Your fantasies forever have been haunted
By dreams that on some future day you might . . .
Now you've got it, go on, flaunt it.

Young you rarely stood up and jaunted
As you groped vainly for the light.
This is something you've always wanted.

I don't mean become a boor and vaunt it
From the top spire of a steeple's height.
But, now that you've got it, do go and flaunt it.

So many centuries you were taunted
Kept in the dark about your plight.
This is something you've always wanted

Now that you've got it, flaunt it.

GALLOPING GUN
(a ghazal—aa, ba, ca, da)

This is a tale of the golden West—a man toting a gun
He has the whole town gnawing its nails—or just about everyone

He swaggers, spurs jangling, into the bar, downs a shot of moonshine
The sheriff, poor fellow, pees in his drawers, and disappears on the run

A boy passing by, races off toward the church to inform the pacifist parson
"Come quick to the Sassy Saloon, Mr. Jack, something awful's going on"

The gunman lays his colt on top of the bar and whoops out a dare
"I'm a gallopin' gringo, the meanest and roughest under Wyoming sun."

"Anybody fool enough to shoot it out with me just stand up and holler
I'd love to blast your britches off, 'cause that's my idee of real fun"

At a table in the corner sits a lone pretty girl with a flask of French wine
Skirt from Nordstrom's, jacket from Saks, not a thing homespun

Her tressess are hidden in a witch's tuck, her stogie belches red fire
Her voice is like a thunderbolt, you can see this is no cloistered nun

She sets down her flask, plants boots to the boards, and calls out to Bully
"I remember you," her words ricochet, "you're Beulah's youngest son

"Stash away that hot toy and stop acting like a television Soprano
It's time to cut hay. Get home to the ranch. They're putting up fifty ton."

Hand at right hip, wad into spittoon, he takes two steps forward
"Don't no women-folk tell me what to do, jist git out of my face, hon"

I can't continue creating more scenes for this chunk of folklore
Not enough words in the rhyming dictionary end with the syllable *un*

To get this far I've made outrageous rhymes about our fabled golden West
I've used every verbal trick I know except for the everyday pun

But moviebuffs know how this Wild Western tale will unravel on from here
That guy and that gal will fall madly in love before the thing is done

And that's how Hollywood makes Western films, something like this
One tough guy, one pretty girl, and one galloping gun

NO COUNTRY FOR OLD MEN
(a pantoum)

> *That is no country for old men. The young*
> *In one another's arms, birds in the trees...*
> William Butler Yeats

After dinner—after the turkey, cranberry sauce and the pumpkin pie
After the young couple had drifted off together into one another's arms
The old man took off on a stroll near the pond, silent—all alone
The thirsty brown banks were showing, the drought taking its toll

After the young couple had drifted off together into one another's arms
They had met on pilgimage, walking together halfway across Spain
The thirsty brown banks were showing, the drought taking its toll
He stood alone at water's edge watching the silken ripples drifting in

They had met on pilgrimage, walking together halfway across Spain
She was European—he had invited her to come meet his family
He stood alone at water's edge watching the silken ripples drifting in
Little green specks of algae had begun growing in the shallows

She was European—he had invited her to come meet his family
All agreed that was brave; for that step, most young men will wait
Little green specks of algae had begun growing in the shallows
Suddenly he was startled by the heavy rustle of feathered wings

All agreed that was brave; for that step, most young men will wait
Like the others, he had fallen in love with the shy young lady from afar
Suddenly he was startled by the heavy rustle of feathered wings
A pair of mallard ducks with much loud quackeroo came floating by

Like the others, he had fallen in love with the shy young lady from afar
She was off somewhere—doubtless in her youthful lover's arms
A pair of mallard ducks with much loud quackeroo came floating by
Abruptly, wings pounding like hammers, they lifted noisily into the sky

She was off somewhere—doubtless in her youthful lover's arms
The old man was off on a stroll near the pond, silent—all alone
A pair of mallard ducks with much loud quackeroo came floating by
After dinner—after the turkey, cranberry sauce and the pumpkin pie

LET'S MAKE A DATE
(a sestina)

Writing a sestina is just a form of college play
I'm about to undertake after dialing you all day
burning up the phone lines attempting my call.
Now it's evening and I am still not getting through.
I feel exhausted and am ready to call it off
because it's clear, today we were not intended to meet.

Heavy dates are not my bag. I need to save and mete
what little energy I have for my goal of playing
soccer. I'm passionate about making it through
the tryouts and to play varsity so that girls will call
me Superstar. But just now after heavy practice all day
I'm ready to call this attempt to make a date with you off.

You must have accidentally left the receiver off
the hook. Connected, we might have talked all through the day
which is a poor substitute for a warm in-person meeting
though some people regard phoning an adequate form of play.
But not me. I wanted you in person. Not just as a telephone call
but to come with me to that party my roommate yesterday threw.

Yesterday a big clumsy athlete dashing through
the fitness-center halls, accidently knocked off
its pedestal the statue of our coach without issuing a call
for help. If he had called, lucky guy, he might have met
you and some of your fellow-actors in the current school play
and you could have all gone off together to celebrate the day.

Looking back on it now I see this has been a wasted day
in which I tried and tried and finally threw
away many wonderful hours. I'd rather be playing
soccer with my buddies. Now I'm going to get off
the phone and surrender my intention of finally meeting
the girl of my dreams. At least I'll no longer keep trying to call.

And yet despite what I've said, here I am making one last call
even though it's been a long and arduous day
during which I dreamed you and I would have a passionate meeting.

68

Unfortunately we never did get through
so now, full of disappointment and sadness, I'm taking off
to give myself over to soccer—to manly, more strenuous play.

Now that we've played telephone tag all day
Calling and calling, never actually getting through
I repeat, let's call it off. This wasn't our day to meet.

THE EMPEROR
(a sestina)

I'd stop just before going into a house
and be an emperor for a minute.
William Stafford

It's that easy. You don't need a golden crown
Or a strongbox full of doubloons and glittering jewels.
You don't need estates tilled by tormented slaves
Or armed legions based on battleships, nukes and tanks.
You don't need any of those. You just need to stop
Denying. Remember who you are: You are an emperor.

All your life you've dreamt of being an emperor.
If only you could be chief honcho wearing a crown.
Then living would be so easy. You could stop
Just admiring, and move on to owning, steep banks of jewels
Under guard at Fort Knox by giant Sherman tanks
And cut and polished to perfection by submissive slaves.

You gaze at the world—what a host of believing slaves!
You're itching to set them free—if you were just emperor.
Toasts. Tidal waves of champagne in overflowing tanks.
Gourmet feasts. Prancing and dancing. And at the crown
Of evening each woman a princess in a gown of jewels.
A night of rapture that keeps going without a stop.

But you know, when sober, this dreaming has to stop.
You know that we human beings must not stay slaves
To fantasy—to feasting, fingering imaginary jewels
Ignoring hard stubborn facts while playing emperor.
You did not win the marathon, were not awarded a crown
of laurel...
            Oh no? Says who? I insist on filling my tanks

With champagne. I'll command the battleships, nukes and tanks
Of my remembered empire. I am a poet! All I need do is stop
For a minute before the house! And remember that fabled crown
I wore when I was master of this multitude of slaves.
You do it too! Just stay and poetize about being emperor.
Then your mind, your page, will be studded with glittering jewels.

70

Diamonds, rubies, amethysts—all manner of imagined jewels.
Imagined mountains of them stored in imaginary tanks
Under command of you, the imaginary emperor.
And don't believe them when they tell you this has to stop.
Hard stubborn facts are domain of servile slaves
Not of poets inspired when wearing the fantasy crown.

All moments are sacred jewels when we remember to stop
And release them from fact-filled tanks tended by slaves.
I wake up! I am emperor! I am reclaiming my rightful crown!

SPURIOUS

Unwilling to frame his thoughts in cool clear prose
The young poet uses phrases and images snappy
But often the result of such arduous labor is sloppy
A bundle of words that cause his readers to doze

He studies rock music searching for highs and for lows
Words that will sound to his readers as if he is zippy
Words like *like* and *man* and *cool* to make him seem hippy
Meanwhile in the depths of his ripening soul he certainly knows

Zip and snap and similar sounds loud and uproarious
Are just noise in the air, made to conceal youthful fears

We boast, make war, compete, live lives fast and furious
Running hard to keep up with our friends of similar years

But with age and wisdom, we see that so much was spurious
Now we smile—we are who we are—despite oceans of tears

ELEGY FOR eMAC

The years pass the wheels turn
Time's forces take their toll.
Please don't call this tragedy
It is not a stake in my soul.

And yet

You've been my friend, my help, my slave
I don't discard you without regret;
But much as I'm attached to you
hard facts demand that I let

you pass to wherever that bleak place is
that's grave for electronic tools.
You've become no longer an asset
You're now a rock in the road for fools

like me, who depend on their computer.
I need sharp salutes and clicked heels
of the flunkeys who handle my copy
without concern from *me* how *they* feel.

I've been giving you years of chances;
You've been failing that awesome test.
So now I've bowed to what has to be
I'm doing what my mind says is best.

You're just a machine, a thing without soul
Just a collection of plastic and wires.
No call for me to be mourning for you
That's more than this situation requires.

And yet, seeing you, your fire eye now blind
Your ports, keys and guts disconnected
No matter what my brain seems to say
In my heart I am deeply affected.

Old friend, confidante, unflappable slave
Let's not despair over this dismal situation
For with recycling now on everyone's lips
We may still meet in another incarnation.

THIS FARM
(for Anna and Anthony)

Carved
  like a statue of polished granite
  from still-untamed wilderness
  of arm-waving, heaven-seeking woods
  rank, uninhibited rampant deer
  and sly snakes lurking under fieldstones
these few just-slightly-fertile hillside acres
  have served
  as home
  as refuge
  as base of operations
  and even as final resting place
for generations
  of simple rural folk
  who lived on and off the land—
  earlier streams of the still-unstanched flood
  of diverse distressed immigrants
  who have created America

Today
  the wilderness, tamer
  the deer, more numerous
  the snakes still sly and lurking
these same hillsides are serving
  as home
  as refuge
  as base of operations
for us new generations
  of immigrants
  offspring of immigrants
  friends of immigrants
grafting
  our young and tender stems
  onto the embedded roots
  of those folk who came before us

Still polishing the granite
  still taming the wilderness
  still creating and
  re-creating America

CICADAS

Ci
        ca   *buzz*

      das   trillions   *snap*
swat   filling
                  the air

     late
spring
        one   *land*
short
                        month
     every
           seventeen
years
               buzz   with song

The earth
     still alive   *slam*
          despite
assaults from
     bulldozers tarmac concrete poisongas skyscrapers missles and
bombs

Each creature
      shouting
    its name   *zzzzz*
                  the livelong
       day   *bang*
   to other
       admiring
             or   *swat*
     indifferent

lookalikes

Trillions
        shouting

                  allatonce

No way   *bang*
       to tell
              one
                  from another
                            swat
"Here I am"
              "Look at me"

"Here I am"

Just like
                  us
                     gottem
people

GARBAGE DISPOSAL

I've never grown comfortable
Living with a garbage disposal
Built into the kitchen sink
Where it groans and rasps
Like an enraged lion
As it devours apple offal
Orange peels and broccoli stems
To turn them into fine-grained mush
That gets flushed uselessly
Into the sewage system
Or with white plastic kitchen bags
For storage of same until
They can be set out in the back alley
On Monday and Thursday afternoons
Along with crushed gift boxes
Crinkled wrapping paper
And other assorted trash
For municipal pickup
By brawny and usually-jolly men
On Tuesday and Friday mornings

In the country
Without such urban gadgetry
Winter or summer
We simply opened the back door
And heaved the garbage out—
Fluttering of wings
Cackling of hens
Scratching and pecking
An occasional bird-biddie-fight
Less harmful than most
People-biddie-fights—
And in a few minutes
All the vegetable detritus
Fit for a hungry-bird meal was gone
To be ground noiselessly
In invisible gizzards
And turned into dinner roasts
And breakfast eggs

Whose yolks slept soundlessly
And when exposed
Smiled into our well-nourished faces
Like the morning sun

AUTUMNAL EQUINOX

Sun rises late in the morning sky
Daylight hours on the wane
Leisurely afternoons cut short
Shadows long on the lane

Yellowed leaves tumble from yawning trees
Frost crystals fringe the pool
Though days are still sunny, mellow, bright
Evenings feeling cool

Cricket-chirp loses late-summer punch
Blackbirds assemble and swarm
Feelings of weariness, harvest, finis
Settle with dusk on the farm

Boom of school buses—the urban world
Vacation trips behind us
But we have miles to go before we sleep
The stern voice of duty reminds us

Happy holidays on the brink
Hallowe'en, Rosh Hashana, Thanksgiving
Campaigning will pass, election will pass
Then we'll resume normal living

We call it Equinox, but here on Earth
We might call it New Year's Day
The sun among sister-stars takes a turn
We turn in our own human way

FIFTEEN WAYS OF LOOKING AT DEER

Being American he mourns the absence
of open space where buffalo roam
and the antelope play with the deer

Along with spring buds and flowers arrive
two long-legged delicate brown-spotted
recently-delivered baby deer

From his seat in the shade he sits entranced
watching as green apples fallen under a tree
are being gobbled up by eager deer

Inspecting the blunt stumps and ragged stems
of the columbines he has raised from seed
he curses the visit last night of the deer

Around the veggies he has toiled to raise
he erects a seven-foot-high fence
to keep out the lazy marauding deer

Skin itching with fire and head a cauldron of heat
he cannot see the black blob of a venomous tick
hidden in the beautiful brown fur of the deer

In his nest in the crotch of a locust tree
he slowly raises his rifle to his eye and
aims at the head of the leading buck deer

From the bloodstained bed of the pickup
he helps unload his friend's winter meat supply
the fresh still-warm carcass of a deer

Over the peak of the rusty barn roof arise
the wide flapping wings of a hungry vulture
on the trail of tasty leftovers of dead deer

In his friend's bedroom he expresses admiration
for the marksman's trophies of the hunt
the stuffed heads of two big buck deer

In the treetop he hears the repeated insistent
calls of birds he cannot name but notes they seem
no threat to the otherwise-ever-suspicious deer

Taking timeout in the heat and hush of mid-July
for the peace of an afternoon nap he remains
oblivious to the languid wanderings of the deer

Standing in the cool waters of the purling stream
as it washes loose pebbles and sand he silently
welcomes an approaching herd of thirsty deer

As they leap away from his sight springing
like floating clouds over hedges and fences
he admires the upright white tails of the deer

And wishes them well

SALUTE TO MY COWS

Empresses of emerald pastures
pampered princesses of the palace called the farm
your sole function to eat and turn fodder into milk—
Belatedly, I salute you.

Mary, my one-horned brindled chamberlain
though you could never negotiate a left-hand turn
you made yourself herd boss, deferred to by all ranks—
Belatedly, I salute you.

Robin, our unacknowledged powerhouse
twice a day you overflowed the milk pail
but it was I who accepted the honor earned by you—
Belatedly, I salute you.

Rosie, sweet heifer named for my beloved sister
I had such high hopes for you—until accidentally you
ripped open your udder on a barb of the wire fence–
Belatedly, I salute you.

Juliana, swift-running mind in the sluggish body of a cow
in your eyes I perceived un-cow-like understanding
and now I forgive your continued AWOL's—
Belatedly, I salute you.

Addie, so pleasant to look at but so foolishly behaved
a great milk producer—except that time you made
a pig of yourself, suffered bellyache and went dry—
Belatedly, I salute you.

Lucelia, noble old lady of the milking stable
you had seen it all—were weary of it all—and yet
you maintained your nobility and served to the very end—
Belatedly, I salute you.

Ladies, on the surface you belonged to me
but beneath the surface I belonged as much to you—
mutual, as real relationships should always be—
Belatedly, I salute you.

Ladies, with your big black uncomprehending eyes
your capacious bellies housing four stomachs each
your half-ton of beef (not the best quality) on the hoof
your gentleness (unless your calf was being threatened)

Ladies, as lowly cows, you could never have known
you were Amazing Grace, saving a wretch like me
helping a blind young man to see—
Belatedly, I salute you.

IN DEFERRAL

Like snowflakes in a windswept flurry
Squirrels are forever rushing
Aways in a hurry.

This fleet-footed squirrel
Is hustling; he has
No interest in deferral.

He is munching seeds
As if they were there
Just for *his* needs

And not to become trees.
His prime concern is *now*.
And yet, like honeybees

He does mind tomorrow
And lays up supplies
To avert future sorrow.

Nuts, fruit, a maple samara—
He'd rather stash those
Than a diamond tiara.

For next winter he'll bury
In this autumn's soil
All the food he can carry.

But after all's frozen
And hard to dig up
He'll foresake the spot chosen.

Not one for self-pampering—
"Gotta root elsewhere"—
Right away he'll go scampering.

Like snowflakes in a windswept flurry
Squirrels are forever rushing
Always in a hurry

HIGHLIGHT

The highlight
of a visit to the farm
in summer
comes on a walk through the meadow

after it has gotten quite dark
when the fireflies
floating over grass and trees
are on full alert.

Gentle fireworks—
twinkling stars—
emerging and fading
steady   steady

within the cosmic blackness
the on-off blinking
constant, unwavering, soundless
in the engulfing spatial gloom

untouched by human presences—
on and off, on and off—
until later into the night
than I am capable of . . .

The highlight comes when visitors
from the city that never sleeps
denizens of Times Square
where bright lights are never dimmed

stop suddenly
wordless
unmoving in their tracks

BEHOLD

then softly whispering
"oohs" and "ahs" in amazement—
never before having witnessed
a spectacle so full of wonder.

IN THE BEGINNING

"You must not do schoolwork or ride your bike
on Saturday," my mother said in Yiddish. "It's Shabbos."
But Jerry and Frank and Fred all wrote lessons
and rode bikes on Saturday—it wasn't sabbath

for them, and nobody ever made it clear to me why
it should be for me. "No argument, just do as I say."
But she was Old World and I was New. So I broke
the rules although I never dared confess it at home.

That was in the beginning.

I won a scholarship to a small Methodist college
where classes were routinely scheduled for Saturdays
and on Sundays we had compulsory chapel.
No protests. At that time nobody protested. Besides

we could not have paid for me to go anywhere else.
I sang Methodist hymns. "This is my Father's world."
And Dr. Holloway preached about God and Jesus
in English—a language I could understand.

No one listened more keenly than I.

The sermons were about God's commandments—
what we *should* do and what we *should not* do.
I skimmed over the parts about Jesus. He was just
another Hebrew prophet—the Torah was full of them.

He didn't seem concerned about my studying
or riding on Shabbos. I concluded he just wanted me
to love God and be good. So much simpler than
what my Jewish mother had demanded of me.

At least, that's what I thought at the time.

BIRTHDAY WITH MOMMA

Momma
I just had a birthday
which makes me now twice as old as you were
when you departed.

That bare wheelchair.
That sorry nursing home. Those derelicts
rotting away like unloved discarded
trash. That stench.

That callow self-centered
boy who resisted visiting there.

Now your photograph
sitting in that same shabby wheelchair
in that same nursing home
watching me as I go back and forth
in my little living room.

So many birthdays
in this same living room—and
you still watching me from the same wheelchair.

Why was that boy not there
for you? And why were you not there for him?
Why did we so fail one another? Why? Why?

After so many years, after
so many crossings in front of
that living-room photograph I still am bound
as in steel by those faraway events.

An innocent ignorant boy. An invalid
mother. Is there ever an answer to why?

Momma,
from your wheelchair in that old photograph

do wish me a happy birthday.

SUNDAY SABBATH
(for Mel Gravitz)

What did I know?what did I know
of love's austere and lonely offices?
Robert Hayden

On Saturdays
from morning till midnight
my father toiled
in his barbershop on The Block
trimming hair, shaving beards
and powdering faces
to make flush customers
look, smell and feel
cleaner and lovelier.

Like other Jews in America
who were poor—
and unlike his less limited
Creator,
Whom he worshiped
formally
only on the holiest holidays—
he observed the weekly Sabbath
resting
not on Saturday
but on Sunday.

Except

the first Sunday of every month
when he collected his clippers,
razors, perfumes and powders
and labored a long day
as a volunteer at Levindale
cutting hair, shaving faces
and making lovelier
those old and disabled residents
who were even poorer.

POPPA'S EXILE

Now, after so many decades
  you long gone
  I an old man
Only now does it occur to me

Poppa

To wonder about your departure
  from your parents
  as a teen-age boy
Into what turned out to be
  permanent exile

What was that scene like?
Were your parents sobbing
  or standing silent at the front door?
Did they wave goodbye?

Did you promise you would write
  from the Goldene Medina?
Did you promise
  that one day you would visit?
  that one day you would send for them
  or maybe some day you'd go back?

Did your mother weep?
Did she kiss you?
Did your father lift his hand
  in a masculine goodbye gesture
  even in that Old World stetl
  as you boarded the little cart
  with your threadbare little bag?

Poppa
  as a child
  I never knew you
Only now that I'm old
  can I begin
  to get acquainted

WOMEN

Women

Young shapely girls

Flowers with beautiful colors and shapes
God created to attract bees

That even Matisse
into his last invalid years
still delighted in painting

Beautiful sexy
hair eyes skin lips neck shoulders
breasts bellies butts
thighs and toes
and all the rest

In my day I've plucked a few
and as an old man
I can still fantasize

I'd love to memorialize
more
in poems

But having grown up Jewish
I feel inhibited

This is as close as I can get

Writing any closer
would feel unkosher

MY FATHERS'S VISIT

At college
I dreaded that one day my father
might decide he'd like to visit
his youngest son
the only member of the clan
to get that far

The professors in their tweeds
the country boys
the pretty shicksas in their fuzzy sweaters
  and saddle shoes
the beautiful campus in its country setting
  green vines climbing
  all over the redbrick walls

I dreaded that my father
with his unreconstructed Yiddish accent
his worn disheveled clothes
his slovenly posture of defeat
might one day decide
he'd like to visit

He never did
and I was relieved

All that was over 60 years ago
It took all that many years
before I made the connection

That man
I called defeated
whose visit I so dreaded
was the same man
who fell dead on the street
pushing his pushcart
in order to put bread on the table
for his wife and kids like me

This is a hurried note
I am out the door
on the way to his shul—
the one he attended
that I do not—
to say Kaddish
in memory of my Poppa

ROSH HASHANA MORNING

and I have been too unconcerned to notify my class
that I would be absent, celebrating this high holiday in shul.
So just now I am preparing
what I will teach in my class.

Harry calls to wish me a Happy New Year. L'Shana Tova.
He is feeling good. He is enrolled at Etz Chaim
a Jewish study group
and is preparing to celebrate the holiday.

I ask him, "Harry, are you into God?"

"Well, I'm into Judaism
so I guess that means I'm into God."

I say, "Harry, I've interviewed too many Holocaust survivors
to be into God."

"Why, aren't they into God?"

"Many aren't. They ask, 'Where were you, God?
How could you have let something like that happen?'
No, many are not into God.

"And on TV I have seen too many children
in Africa starving to death
their little emaciated bodies hardly containing the bones
that are trying to prick their way through the tightly-stretched skin.

"And I've seen too many innocent people
being hacked to pieces with machetes.

"If there is a God,
where, outside the walls of Etz Chaim,
has he been keeping himself?

"Now, Harry, I enjoyed talking to you. Thanks
for wishing me a Happy New Year. I
wish you the same. But I can't
talk to you much longer.
I have to get ready for my class."

YOM KIPPUR

And now Rosh Hashana is behind us
and we see Yom Kippur coming up just ahead.
The holiest day in the Jewish year.
The Day of Atonement,
The day of fasting,
of scrutinizing your life
of critiquing the community's life.

I like that—*the community's life.*
For, one thing Jews are aware of: we are all in it together.
You don't exist without being part of some community.
You may feel like an individual, alienated from it all
but deep inside you know that isn't so. You belong
somewhere even if it is among the community of the godless.

So as you relive horror stories of yesterday's Holocaust
and you survey atrocities going on in the world today
and you ask yourself
Where was God then?
Where is God now?
of course, you are compelled to wonder.

And yet, here is Yom Kippur
coming up just ahead.
The Day of Atonement.
The day of fasting.
The holiest day in the Jewish year.
What wll you do about it?
How will you celebrate it?

You *will* celebrate.
You will ignore the question
of whether God is absent or whether he is present.

You will attend shul. You will fast.
You will immerse yourself in the chanting of prayers.

Not because you have come to rejoice over God's presence.
And not because you have quit complaining about his absence.
You will do those things because on Yom Kippur
that is what a person descended from Abraham, Isaac and Jacob
Does.

BLESSINGS

I've been sitting downstairs
   while waiting for the house to warm up
reading some Hebrew blessings
that Margaret copied off the Internet
   and brought to class as writing exercises.

There is a morning blessing
   for that moment
   when one's eyes first come open:

Modeh ani l'fanecha
melech chai v'kayam
sheheche zarta bi nishmati
b'chemla rabah emunatecha

I give thanks before You
living and eternal King
who has returned my soul into me
in compassion; great is Your faithfulness.

There are other blessings for the seemingly
   mundane activities of dailiness:
     on washing the hands
     on returning from the bathroom
     on breaking bread
all mindful, all sensitive, all enhancing human life.

How wonderful, at this moment
   in a world dripping with hatred and slaughter
that here in this unblemished land
   still in tune with its own convictions
   of tolerance, learning and friendliness
that I, a lapsed, unobservant
   renegade, oldering, Jewish man
   should be teaching and learning
   about English poetry
   at a Catholic college for young women
where an oldering fellow-teacher-learner
   who happens to be Catholic

is introducing me to glorious blessings
   gleaned via the computer
from the Hebrew prayer book
   which is part of my own inheritance.

GROWING UP

When I was growing up
I was blind. Saw
neither trees nor grass
neither family nor friends.
Enveloped in darkness.

A painter taught me
to see. At the easel before
colored canvas I discerned
purples and greens
circles and squares.

When I was growing up
I was mute. Repeated
no tales, whispered
no secrets. Soft tender
lips together sealed.

A singer taught me
to speak. Chanting names
of people and places
actions and things
I was granted a voice.

When I was growing up
my fingers were stone.
Nothing warm or cold
dead or alive
broke into my being.

Loving taught me
to touch. A person—
a dog a cat a horse a place.
Grateful fuzz behind ears.
Electric shock on soft warm skin

When I was growing up
our house had no mirrors.
Eyes, nose, forehead
mouth and chin—
what did I look like?

An old scholar taught me
how to answer that.
Simply held up a glass
for me to look within.
Yes, the likeness is me.

Now I am partly grown up and
I see the past was my teacher.
Making contact with the world
recognizing my face in the glass
I was becoming a poet.

I WAKE UP IN THE MORNING EARLY

I wake in the morning early
And always, the very first thing,
I poke out my head and I sit up in bed
And I sing and I sing and I sing.
                        Rose Fyleman

I wake up in the morning early
No, I usually sleep a bit late
Then I lie back in bed, bobble the brains in my head
And give three cheers for my fortunate Fate

I wake up in the morning early
I have plans for how I'll spend the day
I'll vacuum and make order, take a trip to the border
But my plans seldom come out that way

I wake up in the morning early
My telephone rings off the hook
My friend is in trouble, lost it all in the housing bubble
But I'm confident he's in no way a crook

I wake up in the morning early
The sun is poking in the door
So much on my plate, I'm getting started too late
At thIs rate I'll remain forever a boor

I wake up in the morning early
My eyeglasses are needing repair
But it's out of my way, I'll not get there today
Today I need to go cut my hair

I wake up in the morning early
The teacup I set down last night
Is still nearly half full and I'm as mad as a bull
I'm still sleepy, I'll turn out the light

I wake up in the morning early
The scissors are still on my desk
I slash my pet giraffe and then have a horselaugh
That scares me, it's a bit too grotesque

TRAVEL POSTER

Big-eyed startle-faced
little old me
A new travel poster
and what do I see?

Big Ben towering
over old London town
Saint Buddha taming
a bloodthirsty hound

The Up Eiffel Tower
down in old Paree
A muezzin praying
on low bended knee

The step-sided pyramid
of the god Quetzlcoatl
A pirate three-master
confined in a bottle

In China a succession
of blue-roofed pagodas
In India diapered fakirs
sitting in the lotus

Massive temple columns
in Egyptian Thebes
Sir James Higginbotham
with his old butler Jeeves

The blue and white roof
of the Russian-bear Kremlin
Good riddance to Stalin
and the Communist gremlin

Mao's Great Wall—
of course, he didn't build it
The great river Yangtze
that he's now making silted

This wanderlust of mine—
this thirsting to be traveling—
is making me lubricious
my youthful mind's unraveling

Put me any old somewhere
just not same boring here
I'm still young   not yet sick
with old-people's fear

Give me a rub
at that lamp of Al-adin
a magic carpet flight
that my green heart would gladden

Load me on a rocket
put me on a freighter
an around-the-world cruise
bill my dad for it later

I'm sick of these French verbs
and old English syntax
a course in vagabonding
is what this staid college lacks

Now take down that poster
it's all money-making bluster
to rattle empty heads
to keep uncooked minds a-fluster

Nothing wrong with wanderlust
strange places beneath the sun
sure—THIRST and dream and rub the lamp
But FIRST—get that paper done

WET SHOES

Gurgly
   soaked leather belching
   squishing
   surrendering shape and shine
   so treasured by parents

Kids caught
   in a sudden shower
   and too ornery
   to turn back or go indoors
   just keep playing

In the rain
   not cold rain but
   wet aromatic summer rain
   raindrops pelting
   big as golf bells

Not that hard
   but we feel each one
   as it clunks on cheeks and hands
   Plunk   Plunk   Plunk
   Oh, our new leather sneakers

We kids call them tennis shoes
   and they are not made of leather
   but of canvas
   and we wear them all summer and
   they sprout holes in their sides

So you can see
   our bare soles and toes
   and when it rains
   and the gutters are full of water and
   whatever trash has gathered there

We kids
   in our holy sneakers
   come courageously sloshing through

like conquering cowboys
on sweating steeds

And finally back home
our parents are so relieved
to see we're safe
that they never scold us
for wearing wet shoes

A CHINESE RESTAURANT IN HAMPDEN

Children
Little children
Adorable little Chinese children
Bangs, crew-cuts, pony-tails
Eating at a counter with chopsticks from white plastic bowls

Watching on a computer screen
a big good-natured green dragon named Alfie
driven by a sassy brown-billed bird named Burt
over a caption in strange purple characters
that have to be Chinese

In the dining area Chinese adults on the move
writing orders on palm-sized white pads
speaking in unknown tongues over telephones
delivering meals to hungry seated customers
never standing still in one place

Adorable little Chinese children
when you're older and all grown-up
reading and speaking English
hardly still comprehending Chinese
all melted down into middle America

Will you remember those Chinese adults
running and writing and delivering
not standing still a minute—in order to bring you
that big good-natured green dragon named Alfie
driven by that sassy brown-billed bird named Burt?

Will you remember them?

BALLET
(for Gloria)

High culture, art, exuberant youth
The ballet troupe that danced last night
First, classic sylphs in tutus white
Angels floating in effulgent light
Then drumbeats, flesh—the dance uncouth

From dream-like fairyland to actual
Too tender for this tenacious world
Flowers unfolding petals curled
Lissome pixies gently twirled
Then transformed into factual

Remnants from past stages royal
Apex of choreographic art
Dance into this viewer's heart
At close, regret it's not the start
To you, Ballet, I'll now be loyal

MY(?) MOTHER'S CANDLESTICKS

(a poem for a precious possession)

Are those your mother's candlesticks—
brass and wax and half-burned wicks—
remains of Sabbath candles glowing
Illuminating brightly painted bricks

with pix of pressured peasants sowing
seeds of grass they'll soon be mowing
when they're not eating their salami
and onions that they dream of hoeing?

One of them claims he's a real-life swami—
turban, robes and manner clammy
blessing friends like a born fanatic
and cursing foes with a double whammy.

A poem has gotta have some conflict.
To offset candles, it needs a mix
of sausage, sauerkraut, hicks and mystics.
All this brought on by those candlesticks

that I thought belonged to your late Momma
around which I imagined grimmest drama.

But they are not my mother's candlesticks.
They are not—no way!—*her* candlesticks.

LIMERICK—JOHN UPDIKE

The American author, John Updike
Treated both God and sex just alike
He found it incomprehensible
To not see both indispensable
In the darkness a bright lightning strike

That movie, "The Witches of Eastwick"
Is one helluvan erotic flick
Our library doesn't carry it
The church would like to bury it
Fun with sex—it's gotta be sick

John Updike, while he was dying
Never resorted to crying
He wrote poems every day
So much still to say
No matter that no one was buying

SEVEN AND FOUR

He's seven, in the second grade and sweet.

He's learning "Two plus two" and proudly confronts
the gray-haired man passing on the sidewalk.

"How much?"
The man says quietly that it's twenty-two.

"No. Two plus two is four."
"No it's twenty-two."

The exasperated sigh of a boy's self-confident superiority.

"Look. Two plus two is four."
Two little hands go up,
with two little fingers, capped by two little nails,
outstretched in each one.

"Can't you see."

Two fingers in the left hand come forward
followed by two in the right. The hands
are now side by side.
The abstract made concrete.
"Two plus two is four."

"No. You've got it wrong. These two
alongside these other two make twenty-two."
The man draws two *two's* parallel in the air.
The abstract made imaginary.

The sigh of exasperation is now a clear sign of disgust.

"You're silly...Maybe when *you* went to school...
But now two plus two is four."

"No, you're the silly one. Two plus two is twenty-two."

The sidewalk debate between youth and age goes on
resuming each time the teasing old man passes by.
Harbinger of unending debates to come.

SONNET FOR RAGS

That strap around your neck, the dangling tags
  Announcing who you are, where you belong
Your thick long hair, for which I name you Rags
  And walk you home with me, a cheerful song

Those glowing eyes, like coals in men of snow
  The flouncy tail wagging your scrawny rump
Those photos on the table make memories flow
  My pulse to skip some beats, my heart to jump

Joyful you were, my little shaggy dog
  And I so proud to make that joy a fact

Younger then, I'd take you along to jog
  In sun and snow, so snug our days were packed

You're now all clear, I still in this earthly fog
  Aching for doggie days I never lacked

MY GRANDDAUGHTER

My friend Grace has just been boasting to me
about her granddaughter Regina who has completed
the book she was writing for the Independence Tea Party.
Replying to my query she informs me Regina is too busy
to consider intimacy, love and marriage and prefers
staying independent so she can acquire beautiful things
and visit civilized places in the world.

Having no grandchildren of my own
this conversation leaves me feeling sinful
for having neglected my biological duty
to father the two-point-plus offspring
needed to maintain our human population.
And since in conversations with elderly friends
this subject keeps recurring I have resolved
to invent a granddaughter of my very own.

Her name will be Hope and she has just completed
her formal studies at a Buddhist Institution in Colorado
where she learned to sit breathing quietly for many hours
feeling liberated from things both beautiful and ugly
to help sharpen her awareness of the joy and pain
of being a human being among other sentient beings
in need of compassion in a difficult uncompassionate world.

She is spending this summer as a volunteer at a home
for indigent old people where she cuts grass
and pulls weeds and helps the (mostly black)
white-coated orderlies position the old
(mostly white) ladies in their decrepit wheelchairs so that
they are not exposed to more sun than is good for them.

In the fall she will travel to Tibet
where she will be an intern at the abbey in Lhasa
where the Dalai Lama lived and presided
before being forced to flee his country.
In two or three years along with a diploma
(penned not on sheepskin but on recycled paper)
she will be awarded an antique begging bowl
that will qualify her to beg as she spreads light and love
in some of the civilized places of the world.

I DON'T WANNA HEAR IT

I don't wanna hear it
    I don't wanna hear it at all
        from anybody

But especially
    I don't wanna hear it
        from my fellow Jews

I don't wanna hear from sneering Jewish lips
    That the *schwartzes* are everywhere—they're taking over
    That the *schwartzes* are being left behind because they don't have
        the IQ
    That they've never learned the work ethic
    That as soon as they get into a position of responsibility they
        become corrupt and blow it
    That now after this election our city is going to be in the hands of
        three female schwartzes

I don't wanna be exposed on TV at the homes of Jewish friends
    To the swill that impersonates news
        on the Fox News Channel
    To the venom that vomits
        from the mouths of the likes of Rush Limbaugh

I don't wanna be informed by Jewish friends
    That illegal immigration is being encouraged by the Democrats
        only because
        after they're here long enough they'll all vote Democratic
    That they come to this country just so their kids can be born here
        and be American citizens
        and then they'll go back where they came from
    That California never belonged to Mexico
        it belonged to Spain
        so they've no right to move in
        and fill it up the way they're doing

I don't wanna hear it
    Cause I've heard it all before
        when I was a young man

Only then what I heard was from Gentiles
        about a minority called Jews
            That they are all money-grubbers and Shylocks
                and so be careful when you're doing business with them
            That they control the banks
                and therefore the whole economy
            That they are clannish
                and if you let one in
                the whole neighborhood
                will soon become a ghetto
            That their real country is only other Jews
                and not the United States
            That it was their ancestors who killed God
                so they can't be trusted

That's the kind of crap I used to hear
        when I was a young man

I didn't wanna hear it then
        from the mouths
        of Gentiles
        about a minority called Jews

And dammit I don't wanna hear
        the same sort of crap
        today
        about other minorities
        from the mouths
        of my fellow Jews

MILTON THE BUDDHIST

Seated on your scarlet and gold zafu
Eyes half-closed, legs crossed, palms up
In a posture of openness to Whatever
You resemble an Egyptian pyramid
Solid, immovable and eternal.
And yet like the great stone pyramids
Patient in the bare and trackless desert
You are indifferent to what others find eternal
For Eternity, you are aware, is Now.

The purple string around your neck
Declares the refuge you have taken
In the Buddha, Master of So Many Millions
In whom you have found a master—
You, who previously could bow down to no one.
Your roots in ancient Judaism
Charging you as healer of the wounds of the world
You have grafted to the tree of Bod Gaya, nourishing
Its green ascent through eternity toward the stars.

No saint, no ascetic, your eternal quip was
"Enjoy the world, just don't get attached to it."
And you enjoyed: Food, nature, friends
Women. With an agile hand you steered
Your ship through the shoals of the stock market.
You loved being enshrined as guru to disciples
Explaining, advising and healing, especially those
Pretty, young and female, on whom your advice
About detachment was eternally wasted.

Today, Old Friend, standing before your horizontal plot
In the veterans' section of the grassy Jewish cemetery
Bare biographical facts engraved in the vertical headstone
Along with a few letters of undecipherable Hebrew—
No note of your body bending humbly before the Buddha—
I recall the litany of your advice about eternity.
I wonder how you might be faring in your stay there
And familiar words of my old comrade come to me.
"Enjoy that world—just don't get attached to it."

PRIME TIME

Let's not let Poppa hurry round the bend.
His wrinkled pose, his lust for solemn crape
His willingness when old to simply scrape
Along toward the date that he must end

His awful readiness to whine and bend
To yield as hasty grandsons ache to drape
His corpse, his bones, his vitals with mourning tape
Is beyond what my poor brain can comprehend.

Keep going the game, take no account of years;
The play will end, but the current scene's sublime.

The last thing we should do is yield to fears,
To leave ere curtain falls would be a crime.

The wonder of each moment is too dear,
Just to breathe and love is still prime time.

MEN FRIENDS

last night with Howard
sitting alongside in the car
city darkness around you
raindrops pummeling the roof
engine-purr silenced
headlights turned off
background sound the on-and-off clicking
  of the rear hazard light

each of you talks
each taking a turn
then waiting for the other
just the two of you
just keep on talking
late into the dark night
right up to where time
  begins moving toward the edge

you talk
of your work
of your families
of your dreams
of being bored
of being scared
of being sometimes depressed
  and how you keep moving on with all that

last night with Howard
sitting alongside in the car
city darkness around you
talking—just talking

this morning pausing to recall
last night's communion
two friends—opening gates
usually closed, to one another

BOXES

In my long lifetime I have lived with many kinds of boxes
Most of them dispensable

The blue-and-yellow cardboard box from Office Depot
That housed three reams of the acid-free aircraft I'm now flying on

The small neat finely-finished wooden box from Korea
That houses 50 bags of ginseng tea which scatter my afternoon clouds

The see-through box in the shape of a friendly fatted pig
That houses my hog-heavy treasure trove of pennies nearly-worthless

The box with inlaid wood ducks I bought long ago in Italy
That houses the few lira and shillings I hoard from a former incarnation

BUT

The box that oppresses my pulse as I sit here scribbling is
The eight-foot-long mahogany box with the cover permanently closed

Which I just touched with my friends Jim and Mary Bready
That houses what 's left of the diseased body of youthful Anne Bready

Wife of devoted Chris and mother of adoring Alexander
Spirited away too soon from the people who loved and needed her

The box that houses a dear faithful family's sorrow and grief
The eight-foot-long mahogany box with the cover permanently closed

THE ASSASSINATION TANGO
(for Robert Duvall after seeing his movie of the same name)

A genie popped out of a bottle one day
Big, dark-eyed, mysterious, like a giant from Bombay.
He said, "Since many years you never flinched from a dare
You can have what you wish for, any time, anywhere.

"Just name it, you've got it," he declared. "Surely you
Have memories from childhood that you'd like to undo
And fantasies, desires, that were never fulfilled.
Now, in your dotage, you can have what you then willed."

Full of wonder, I pondered, a thrumming deep in m soul
Lie a breakfast of cornflakes, stirred around in a bowl
Considered riches, beauty, deep knowledge and glory
But I soon turned from these to a more fabulous story.

I said, "Make me into a tall handsome young guy,
Who's brilliant, a scholar, with renown that's sky-high."
But then it struck me, what I long for, even more than good looks
Is a taste and a skill that I can't learn from books.

"Dancing the Assassination Tango is the ecstasy I dream of.
The way Duvall and partner do it, I know, is the cream of
All the dances I've seen. Genie, give me that present
And I'll give up all regrets for my days pre-pubescent.

"Let me dance with a beautiful long-legged queen
Who will wrap legs around me in ways seldom seen,
Who will glide with soft music and bounce with the beat,
Who will kick high behind me with stilleto-heeled feet.

"Oh, Genie, too long I've pursued thoughts profound,
Intellectual and spiritual while bound with chains to the ground.
Oh, Genie, generous Genie, I am old now and wise.
Just let me dance the Assassination Tango as my prize."

GRACE

My luncheon cheese sandwich.
Two thin slices of bread
lifted frozen from my freezer this morning
a spattering of creamy mayo
a few slices of cheese
crinkly little leaves of unruly lettuce
spilling out over the brown crusts.
A most ordinary simple sandwich..

In her body-mind-spirit lecture this morning
the physician-minister suggested
we should pause a few times each day
to pray.
"Stimulates the endorphins," she said.
"Good for the health."

So
before I savage that most ordinary food morsel
between my eager jaws
as I usually do
I pause and just look at it.
Bread, mayo, cheese, lettuce—so ordinary.

"Say a prayer, Isaac, as the good doctor suggested."
I could say a Hebrew blessing
thanking God for providing us bread
or a Christian grace, invoking the name of Jesus.

Instead

I just sit in silence staring
—for the sake of my endorphins.
Bread, mayo, cheese, lettuce.
To procure that bit of bread
I plowed not one square foot of soil.
To possess those slices of cheese
I milked not a single cow.
I neither sowed nor harvested
that green lettuce leaf

and I'm not even sure of what goodies
constitute the mayo.

I am aware
that for the sake of my health
my mind should be emptied by now.

Instead
it is filled with this thought:
that amid the slaughters and starvations
taking place around us
in this bloody twenty-first century of ours
that by having for my lunch today
this most ordinary of simple sandwiches
I am a member
of the rarest
richest
luckiest minority
on the face of the Earth.

Endorphins, make the most of it.

TO BRING YOU PEACE

To bring you peace we had to invade
No matter how high the price to be paid
Bombers and missiles, destroying all hope
For a peaceful land where families could cope
Without the bomb and grenade

Congress gave our leader an accolade
As if he himself had stormed the barricade
Or climbed his own way up a slippery slope
Or had orders from God relayed through the Pope
To bring you peace

How strange this international masquerade
Where innocence is skived with a whetted blade
Where lynching occurs with ambush, not rope
Where leaders can't say with one voice the word "Nope"
A nasty unending war that was made
To bring you peace

PLEASE GOD LET ME DIE

the way Ted died. This morning
Margie called me—"I just wanted
to inform you. Daddy died
last night." "Oh, Margie
what a beautiful way to die." He lived

into his nineties with little discomfort,
no serious illnesses, in his own house
surrounded by friends, people
who loved him. He had a stroke
spent a few days in the hospital

then to a comfortable nursing home.
Always fully aware. We friends visited him
often, and he carried on conversations
with us, sometimes slurring words
not using his useless left arm

but all of his mental faculties intact.
Margie, who lived in Massachusetts,
came frequently to visit. Vernon came
and brought him whatever he needed
from the house. Margie decided

she needed to move him closer to her
home in Mass. She chartered a special plane
to transport him—that was to be on Monday.
Saturday evening there was a party
for him at the nursing home. Dozens of friends

from the numerous walks of his life came
to pay their respects. Everyone understood
this would be the last time
they would be seeing one another.
The Manor Care staff worked hard

getting him shiny and dressed
so he could attend. He did. He seemed
fully aware, seemed to enjoy every minute of it.

Then he went back to bed, Margie preparing
to take him to the airport Monday morning.

Sunday night he died in his sleep.
"What a beautiful way to die."
This morning, I was still in bed
when Margie called to inform me
and that was my instant instinctive reply.

"What a beautiful way to die." God
You know I don't bother you very often
but there is this one favor I ask:
when it comes my turn please
let me die the way Ted died.

OLD AGE: THE BRIGHT SIDE

Into the darkness of old age and night,
  Gradually drive and ambition fade away
  Along with the chimeras of previous day
Visions of youth that used to dominate the light.

The crush, the confusion, the power, the might
  The vain cheap fanfare and the loud array
  The doubts, the worries, that unceasing lay
Heavily on our souls we see now to be slight.

Intimations of a quieter life: the noise no more
  Annoys us. From afar we hear but can annul
  Its provocation, its offense to peaceful days,

Mere nuisances modern life makes us endure
  As now, at last, we make our lives more graceful
  Pursuing more serene and simple ways.

DAS LAND DER UNBEGRENZTEN MOEGLICHKEITEN
(THE LAND OF LIMITLESS POSSIBILITIES)
(An epithet used by Germans about America shortly after World War II)

A man of color
born and raised in interracial Hawaii
of an African father and a white mother
is elected leader of America
and of the world

A young Chinese woman
with a big toothy smile
whose pronunciation of the word *bagel*
is mutilated almost beyond recognition
is successfully managing a bagel-shop
on a busy street in downtown Baltimore

An elderly Jewish man inside the shop
eating a lox-and-bagel sandwich
notices at the curb out front
a dark-haired woman
in a white head-scarf
anxiously ransacking her purse
for coins to feed a parking meter.
He hurriedly gets change for a dollar bill
from the smiling Chinese manager
and offers the woman quarters
so she can safely leave her car

A classroom full of black students
in a public high-school
who had for months been abstaining
from recitation of the Pledge of Allegiance
today on the morning after the election
spontaneously and enthusiastically
are repeating the pledge
blasting out the final words
like skyrockets on the Fourth of July
"with liberty and justice for all"

LET ME GO

Don't make me another Terry Schiavo
Don't make heroic moves to extend my time
I don't mean to say that you should up and kill me
That would be a crime
But when my time is up, please let me go

At my ripe age I'm full of bodily ills
They cause me pain in places you don't see
But I won't bore you making lists of them—
Let's let them be
I have my doc—he prescribes the needed pills

But don't make me another Terry Schiavo
Show me your love with a kiss and one more hug
Don't keep me breathing if all I'll do is suffer
Be brave: pull the plug
When my time is up will be time to let me go

CHILD COUNSEL

The child, they say, is father of the man—which means
that *little I* must do everything I can
to make your adult life secure and happy
even if sometimes I will come across
as foolish and sappy. Recall the way
I encouraged you at school to study and cram
to please your teachers, and never play the fool
in order that you could be top dog,
head of your class—though
that meant you had to give up pursuing
that raven-headed lass named Susanna
whose love had so moved you
that one fall you said you were about to chuck it all
and run off and marry her. Not the smart thing to do.

You could have been a doctor, a lawyer, an Indian chief—
of course you might have fallen and wound up a thief—
but somehow given the chances life has brought you
you prospered, grew rich, as I always knew you ought to.
And now you're a billionaire, loaded to distraction
with money bags in a gigantic plush suburban McMansion
—with a landscaped yard full of bright waving flags
from strange distant countries that you own parts of.

I hear your complaint.
You say you've never known love.
You say you'd prefer a few words that are not a lie
from one girl who really cared for you to the adoration
of the hundreds you can buy. Big Daddy it's plain
that you're caught in a web of fairy tales
not proper for your station. Though some day, if you're lucky
you may become old enough to read fairy tales again.

As the child you were when we began this expedition
I counsel you: Be real. Be here now. See it as your mission
to enjoy your cars, your yachts, your penthouse
in Djibouti. Stop fretting for the past—
as if you didn't do your duty. Believe me
what counts is being in possession of the manna.

With enough of that you can get any beautiful young Susanna.

And while you're dealing with a plutocrat's unimportant little stresses
forget not, I'm the child who fathered your successes.

IN PRAISE OF LEGS

This year, God, I'm thanking you for legs
all kinds of legs—my own two legs   legs of friends
kids' legs   legs I've fantasized over
and turkey legs I intend very soon to eat

Legs, God, are one of your many unsung glories
remember the envy of that serpent in your garden
for those long strong legs you bestowed on your creature man
while that evil one was cursed to crawl forever in dirt

Full disclosure, God—one pair of legs among my fantasies
these late days are those long sexy gold-stockinged legs
I was fortunate enough to spy in a church hall last spring
and for which I silently begged from you a holy blessing

But onward, God, to my own legs—not what they were
but still doing their job, carrying me almost daily
on a walk through my Medfield neighborhood
where I can watch children on sidewalks disporting legs

God, did you notice that little boy in diapers
feet pounding the pavement like little pistons
on his newly-discovered legs, the sound like a hymn
to you in thanks for those two obedient locomotives

Don't forget, please, God, to bless the weakened legs
in the retirement community my friend Robert lives in—
worn-out legs that depend now on walkers
arthritic legs that yield now to wheelchairs

And thank you, God, for your creations on four legs
dogs   horses   cows   lions   wolves—
and for your equally beautiful creations on six
butterflies   ants   bees   even the stink bugs

Thank you, God, for pairs of legs on birds that fly
for floating fins resembling legs on fish that swim
for the hundred legs commanded by the centipede
and the thousand that move the millipede along

And finally, God, thank you in advance for the robust leg
on that brown roasted turkey I'll be devouring soon
submerged in gravy banked by sweet potatoes
and surrounded by even sweeter family and friends

Praise legs

THANK YOU GOD FOR TUESDAY

Thank you God for Tuesday
On Tuesday I know who I am
That's not true on Monday
or Wednesday or Friday
or either of those long open days
on the weekend.
But on Tuesday I know who I am.

Mondays, Wednesdays, Fridays
et al
I'm a hundred different guys: friend
uncle, landowner, householder
neighbor, leftover brother
son and grandson
heir to a tradition I'm obligated
to follow even when I don't wanna
fellow-American, citizen, voter
Oh, those Mondays, Wednesdays
Fridays
et al
Who in the world are you, Isaac
on those days?

Thursday's OK. On Thursdays
I'm just a student, a member, a playreader
a lunch packer and a lunch companion
a fellow-complainer
Oh, I can handle Thursdays.

But Tuesday—thank you God for Tuesday
On Tuesday I become a prince—a POET
On Tuesday I study with my peers how to read
a poem. I write a poem. I read the poem
I have written. I read and hear poems
by fellow-poets. I'm a scholar acquiring
the wisdom that poetry is., Oh, the wisdom
I acquire just listening in my own class!
So what if much of that wisdom
has just come off the internet—

it comes off channeled to me and through me
the Renaissance coordinator
on Tuesdays.

Thank you God for Tuesday.

IN THE MIRROR

In my bathroom mirror
two faces—
this gray-framed one
and a little wistful-looking boy
that I once knew in East Baltimore

Wistful stares back
at Old Gray

"Who are you anyway?
Are you still doing impersonations?
Who was it today? The teacher? The poet?
The nature-loving farmer? The writer?

"All of them are still me, you know
the little lonely boy you once knew"

I recall that lonely little boy
forever seeking and failing to get the attention
that should be every child's due
I am aware of the unfortunate circumstances
that were making him into a pack of empty yearnings

Yet I did not care for him
I knew sympathy
but I can't say that I ever liked him
What was to like?

But look at him now—
there in the mirror
He has survived
to do impersonations—
writer teacher farmer poet—
and do them well
He seems now a decent adult human being—
even rather happy

People I approve of
approve—
and so do I

I'm really quite proud of him
In fact I've come
to actually like him

ORTHODENTAPHILIA

When things are going wrong
When the whole world's looking blue
When the bad days last too long
And the false beats out the true

When whatever you have started
Seems to end up a big mess
When the more you put into it
It always seems to come out less

When you think it's no more worth it
To keep running the good race
And you want to raise your hands up
And disappear without a trace

And you accept you want to die now
And have your corpse let down beneath
Six feet of heavy green sod—
Have a thought to your own teeth

White crunchers that have served you
Gritty millstones that have ground
Whatever stuff you've fed them
Steaks and nuts that you have downed

Remember when those teeth ached
And the world was colored black
And you felt you were being tortured
Were being stretched thin on the wrack

That was absolute pits-time
No pain could pierce so deep
An elf with a ball-peen hammer
Beating your nerves into a creep

Now—turn and regard the present
Those teeth are not now aching
They're in place, quiet and peaceful
Faithful slaves, yours for the taking

No toothache—is that so?
Those blues I suffered seem paltry
I feel so clean, so relieved
I could go out and climb a tall tree

I'm enjoying orthodentaphilia—
A new word—let me explain
It means I love my own good teeth
It means I've no grounds to complain

It means no toothache—I love it
I feel swell, not the slightest doubt
I look back on what seemed my troubles—
What was that moaning all about?